AF303666

Joyce Marx Emerson Chesterton Cooper Austen
Defoe Abbott Hardy Machiavelli Hugo Grimm
Melville Montaigne Haggard Eliot
Stoker Christie Carroll Molière
Wilde Maupassant Byron Schiller
Garnett Fitzgerald Engels Smith Kafka
Goethe Einstein Hawthorne Hall
Cotton Dostoyevsky Willis
Baum Henry Kipling Doyle
Leslie Dumas Nietzsche
Flaubert Turgenev Balzac
Stockton Vatsyayana Crane
Burroughs Verne
Curtis Tocqueville Whitman Vinci
Homer Widger Tolstoy Gogol Busch
Darwin Thoreau Twain
Potter Freud Zola Lawrence Scott Harte
Kant Jowett Stevenson Dickens Plato
Andersen Hesse
London Descartes Cervantes Burton
Poe Aristotle Wells Voltaire
Hale James Hastings Cooke
Bunner Shakespeare Irving
Richter Chambers
Doré da Shaw Benedict Alcott
Swift Dante Chekhov Wodehouse Pushkin
Newton

 tredition®

tredition was established in 2006 by Sandra Latusseck and Soenke Schulz. Based in Hamburg, Germany, tredition offers publishing solutions to authors and publishing houses, combined with world-wide distribution of printed and digital book content. tredition is uniquely positioned to enable authors and publishing houses to create books on their own terms and without conventional manu-facturing risks.

For more information please visit: www.tredition.com

TREDITION CLASSICS

This book is part of the TREDITION CLASSICS series. The creators of this series are united by passion for literature and driven by the intention of making all public domain books available in printed format again - worldwide. Most TREDITION CLASSICS titles have been out of print and off the bookstore shelves for decades. At tredition we believe that a great book never goes out of style and that its value is eternal. Several mostly non-profit literature projects provide content to tredition. To support their good work, tredition donates a portion of the proceeds from each sold copy. As a reader of a TREDITION CLASSICS book, you support our mission to save many of the amazing works of world literature from oblivion. See all available books at www.tredition.com.

Project Gutenberg

The content for this book has been graciously provided by Project Gutenberg. Project Gutenberg is a non-profit organization founded by Michael Hart in 1971 at the University of Illinois. The mission of Project Gutenberg is simple: To encourage the creation and distribution of eBooks. Project Gutenberg is the first and largest collection of public domain eBooks.

Memoirs of the Courts of Louis XV and XVI. Being secret memoirs of Madame Du Hausset, lady's maid to Madame de Pompadour, and of the Princess Lamballe — Volume 2

Mme. Du Hausset

Imprint

This book is part of TREDITION CLASSICS

Author: Mme. Du Hausset
Cover design: Buchgut, Berlin – Germany

Publisher: tredition GmbH, Hamburg - Germany
ISBN: 978-3-8424-5364-7

www.tredition.com
www.tredition.de

MEMOIRS OF LOUIS XV. AND XVI.

Being Secret Memoirs of Madame du Hausset, Lady's Maid to Madame de Pompadour, and of an unknown English Girl and the Princess Lamballe

BOOK 2.

Madame sent for me yesterday evening, at seven o'clock, to read something to her; the ladies who were intimate with her were at Paris, and M. de Gontaut ill. "The King," said she, "will stay late at the Council this evening; they are occupied with the affairs of the Parliament again." She bade me leave off reading, and I was going to quit the room, but she called out, "Stop." She rose; a letter was brought in for her, and she took it with an air of impatience and ill-humour. After a considerable time she began to talk openly, which only happened when she was extremely vexed; and, as none of her confidential friends were at hand, she said to me, "This is from my brother. It is what he would not have dared to say to me, so he writes. I had arranged a marriage for him with the daughter of a man of title; he appeared to be well inclined to it, and I, therefore, pledged my word. He now tells me that he has made inquiries; that the parents are people of insupportable hauteur; that the daughter is very badly educated; and that he knows, from authority not to be doubted, that when she heard this marriage discussed, she spoke of the connection with the most supreme contempt; that he is certain of this fact; and that I was still more contemptuously spoken of than himself. In a word, he begs me to break off the treaty. But he has let me go too far; and now he will make these people my irreconcilable enemies. This has been put in his head by some of his flatterers; they do not wish him to change his way of living; and very few of them would be received by his wife." I tried to soften Madame, and, though I did not venture to tell her so, I thought her brother right. She persisted in saying these were lies, and, on the following Sunday, treated her brother very coldly. He said nothing to me at that time; if he had, he would have embarrassed me greatly. Madame atoned for everything by procuring favours, which were the means of facilitating the young lady's marriage with a gentleman of the

Court. Her conduct, two months after marriage, compelled Madame to confess that her brother had been perfectly right.

I saw my friend, Madame du Chiron. "Why," said she, "is the Marquise so violent an enemy to the Jesuits? I assure you she is wrong. All powerful as she is, she may find herself the worse for their enmity." I replied that I knew nothing about the matter. "It is, however, unquestionably a fact; and she does not feel that a word more or less might decide her fate."—"How do you mean?" said I. "Well, I will explain myself fully," said she. "You know what took place at the time the King was stabbed: an attempt was made to get her out of the Castle instantly. The Jesuits have no other object than the salvation of their penitents; but they are men, and hatred may, without their being aware of it, influence their minds, and inspire them with a greater degree of severity than circumstances absolutely demand. Favour and partiality may, on the other hand, induce the confessor to make great concessions; and the shortest interval may suffice to save a favourite, especially if any decent pretext can be found for prolonging her stay at Court." I agreed with her in all she said, but I told her that I dared not touch that string. On reflecting on this conversation afterwards, I was forcibly struck with this fresh proof of the intrigues of the Jesuits, which, indeed, I knew well already. I thought that, in spite of what I had replied to Madame du Chiron, I ought to communicate this to Madame de Pompadour, for the ease of my conscience; but that I would abstain from making any reflection upon it. "Your friend, Madame du Chiron," said she, "is, I perceive, affiliated to the Jesuits, and what she says does not originate with herself. She is commissioned by some reverend father, and I will know by whom." Spies were, accordingly, set to watch her movements, and they discovered that one Father de Saci, and, still more particularly, one Father Frey, guided this lady's conduct. "What a pity," said Madame to me, "that the Abbe Chauvelin cannot know this." He was the most formidable enemy of the reverend fathers. Madame du Chiron always looked upon me as a Jansenist, because I would not espouse the interests of the good fathers with as much warmth as she did.

Madame is completely absorbed in the Abbe de Bernis, whom she thinks capable of anything; she talks of him incessantly. Apropos, of this Abbe, I must relate an anecdote, which almost makes one believe in conjurors. A year, or fifteen months, before her disgrace, Madame de Pompadour, being at Fontainebleau, sat down to write at a desk, over which hung a portrait of the King. While she was, shutting the desk, after she had finished writing, the picture fell, and struck her violently on the head.. The persons who saw the accident were alarmed, and sent for Dr. Quesnay. He asked the circumstances of the case, and ordered bleeding and anodynes. Just, as she had been bled, Madame de Brancas entered, and saw us all in confusion and agitation, and Madame lying on her chaise-longue. She asked what was the matter, and was told. After having expressed her regret, and having consoled her, she said, "I ask it as a favour of Madame, and of the King (who had just come in), that they will instantly send a courier to the Abbe de Bernis, and that the Marquise will have the goodness to write a letter, merely requesting him to inform her what his fortune-tellers told him, and to withhold nothing from the fear of making her uneasy." The thing was, done as she desired, and she then told us that La Bontemps had predicted, from the dregs in the, coffee-cup, in which she read everything, that the, head of her best friend was in danger, but that no fatal consequences would ensue.

The next day, the Abbe wrote word that Madame Bontemps also said to him, "You came into the world almost black," and that this was the fact. This colour, which lasted for some time, was attributed to a picture which hung at the foot of his, mother's bed, and which she often looked at. It represented a Moor bringing to Cleopatra a basket of flowers, containing the asp by whose bite she destroyed herself. He said that she also told him, "You have a great deal of money about you, but it does not belong to you;" and that he had actually in his pocket two hundred Louis for the Duc de La Valliere. Lastly, he informed us that she said, looking in the cup, "I see one of your friends—the best—a distinguished lady, threatened with an accident;" that he confessed that, in spite of all his philosophy, he turned pale; that she remarked this, looked again into the cup, and continued, "Her head will be slightly in danger, but of this no appearance will remain half an hour afterwards." It was impossible to doubt the facts. They appeared so surprising to the King, that he desired some inquiry to be made concerning the fortune-teller. Madame, however, protected her from the pursuit of the Police.

A man, who was quite as astonishing as this fortune-teller, often visited Madame de Pompadour. This was the Comte de St. Germain, who wished to have it believed that he had lived several centuries.

[St. Germain was an adept — a worthy predecessor of Cagliostro, who expected to live five hundred years. The Count de St. Germain pretended to have already lived two thousand, and, according to him, the account was still running. He went so far as to claim the power of transmitting the gift of long life. One day, calling upon his servant to, bear witness to a fact that went pretty far back, the man replied, "I have no recollection of it, sir; you forget that I have only had the honour of serving you for five hundred years."

St. Germain, like all other charlatans of this sort, assumed a theatrical magnificence, and an air of science calculated to deceive the vulgar. His best instrument of deception was the phantasmagoria; and as, by means of this abuse of the science of optics, he called up shades which were asked for, and almost always recognised, his correspondence with the other world was a thing proved by the concurrent testimony of numerous witnesses.

He played the same game in London, Venice, and Holland, but he constantly regretted Paris, where his miracles were never questioned.

St. Germain passed his latter days at the Court of the Prince of Hesse Cassel, and died at Plewig, in 1784, in the midst of his enthusiastic disciples, and to their infinite astonishment at his sharing the common destiny.]

One day, at her toilet, Madame said to him, in my presence, "What was the personal appearance of Francis I.? He was a King I should have liked." — "He was, indeed, very captivating," said St. Germain; and he proceeded to describe his face and person as one does that of a man one has accurately observed. "It is a pity he was too ardent. I could have given him some good advice, which would have saved him from all his misfortunes; but he would not have followed it; for it seems as if a fatality attended Princes, forcing them to shut their ears, those of the mind, at least, to the best advice, and especially in the most critical moments." — "And the Constable," said Madame, "what do you say of him?" — "I cannot say much good or much harm of him," replied he. "Was the Court of Francis I. very brilliant?"—"Very brilliant; but those of his grandsons infinitely surpassed it. In the time of Mary Stuart and Margaret of Valois it was a land of enchantment—a temple, sacred to pleasures of every kind; those of the mind were not neglected. The two Queens were learned, wrote verses, and spoke with captivating grace and eloquence." Madame said, laughing, "You seem to have seen all this."—"I have an excellent memory," said he, "and have read the history of France with great care. I sometimes amuse myself, not by making, but by letting it be believed that I lived in old times."—"You do not tell me your age, however, and you give yourself out for very old. The Comtesse de Gergy, who was Ambassadress to Venice, I think, fifty years ago, says she knew you there exactly what you are now."—"It is true, Madame, that I have known Madame de Gergy a long time."—"But, according to what she says, you would be more than a hundred"—"That is not impossible," said he, laughing; "but it is, I allow, still more possible that Madame de Gergy, for whom I have the greatest respect, may be in her dotage."—"You have given her an elixir, the effect of which is surprising. She declares that for a long time she has felt as if she was only four-and-twenty years of age; why don't you give some to the King?"—"Ah! Madame," said he, with a sort of terror, "I must be mad to think of giving the King an unknown drug." I went into my room to write down this conversation. Some days afterwards, the King, Madame de Pompadour, some Lords of the Court, and the Comte de St. Germain, were talking about his secret for causing the spots in diamonds to disappear. The King ordered a diamond of middling size, which had a spot, to be brought. It was weighed; and the King said to the Count, "It is valued at two hundred and forty louis; but it would be worth four hundred if it had no spot. Will you try to put a hundred and sixty louis into my pocket?" He examined it carefully, and said, "It may be done; and I will bring it you again in a month." At the time appointed, the Count brought back the diamond without a spot, and gave it to the King. It was wrapped in a cloth of amianthus, which he took off. The King had it weighed, and found it but very little diminished. The King sent it to his jeweller by M. de Gontaut, without telling him anything of what had passed. The jeweller gave three hundred and eighty louis for it. The King, however, sent for it back again, and kept it as a curiosity. He could not overcome his surprise, and said that M. de St. Germain must be worth millions, especially if he had also the secret of making large diamonds out of a number of small ones. He neither said that he had, nor that he had not; but he positively asserted that he could make pearls grow, and give them the finest water. The King, paid him great attention, and so did Madame de Pompadour. It was from her I learnt what I have just related. M. Queanay said, talking of the pearls, "They are produced by a disease in the oyster. It is possible to know the cause of it; but, be that as it may, he is not the less a quack, since he pretends to have the elixir vitae, and to have lived several centuries. Our master is, however, infatuated by him, and sometimes talks of him as if his descent were illustrious."

I have seen him frequently: he appeared to be about fifty; he was neither fat nor thin; he had an acute, intelligent look, dressed very simply, but in good taste; he wore very fine diamonds in his rings, watch, and snuff-box. He came, one day, to visit Madame de Pompadour, at a time when the Court was in full splendour, with knee and shoe-buckles of diamonds so fine and brilliant that Madame said she did not believe the King had any equal to them. He went into the antechamber to take them off, and brought them to be examined; they were compared with others in the room, and the Duc de Gontaut, who was present, said they were worth at least eight thousand louis. He wore, at the same time, a snuff-box of inestimable value, and ruby sleeve-buttons, which were perfectly dazzling. Nobody could find out by what means this man became so rich and so remarkable; but the King would not suffer him to be spoken of with ridicule or contempt. He was said to be a bastard son of the King of Portugal.

I learnt, from M. de Marigny, that the relations of the good little Marechale (de Mirepoix) had been extremely severe upon her, for what they called the baseness of her conduct, with regard to Madame de Pompadour. They said she held the stones of the cherries which Madame ate in her carriage, in her beautiful little hands, and that she sate in the front of the carriage, while Madame occupied the whole seat in the inside. The truth was, that, in going to Crecy, on an insupportably hot day, they both wished to sit alone, that they might be cooler; and as to the matter of the cherries, the villagers having brought them some, they ate them to refresh themselves, while the horses were changed; and the Marechal emptied her pocket-handkerchief, into which they had both thrown the cherry-stones, out of the carriage window. The people who were changing the horses had given their own version of the affair.

I had, as you know, a very pretty room at Madame's hotel, whither I generally went privately. I had, one day, had visits from two or three Paris representatives, who told me news; and Madame, having sent for me, I went to her, and found her with M. de Gontaut. I could not help instantly saying to her, "You must be much pleased, Madame, at the noble action of the Marquis de — — —." Madame replied, drily, "Hold your tongue, and listen to what I have to say to you." I returned to my little room, where I found the Comtesse d'Amblimont, to whom I mentioned Madame's reception of me. "I know what is the matter," said she; "it has no relation to you. I will explain it to you. The Marquis de — — —-has told all Paris, that, some days ago, going home at night, alone, and on foot, he heard cries in a street called Ferou, which is dark, and, in great part, arched over; that he drew his sword, and went down the street, in which he saw, by the light of a lamp, a very handsome woman, to whom some ruffians were offering violence; that he approached, and that the woman cried out, 'Save me! save me!' that he rushed upon the wretches, two of whom fought him, sword in hand, whilst a third held the woman, and tried to stop her mouth; that he wounded one in the arm; and that the ruffians, hearing people pass at the end of the street, and fearing they might come to his assistance, fled; that he went up to the lady, who told him that they were not robbers, but villains, one of whom was desperately in love with her; and that the lady knew not how to express her gratitude; that she had begged him not to follow her, after he had conducted her to a fiacre; that she would not tell him her name, but that she insisted on his accepting a little ring, as a token of remembrance; and that she promised to see him again, and to tell him her whole history, if he gave her his address; that he complied with this request of the lady, whom he represented as a charming person, and who, in the overflowing of her gratitude, embraced him several times. This is all very fine, so far," said Madame d'Amblimont, "but hear the rest. The Marquis de exhibited himself everywhere the next day, with a black ribbon bound round his arm, near the wrist, in which part he said he had received a wound. He related his story to everybody, and everybody commented upon it after his own fashion. He went to dine with the Dauphin, who spoke to him of his bravery, and of his fair unknown, and told him that he had already complimented the Duc de C— — on the affair. I forgot to tell you," continued Madame d'Amblimont, "that, on the very night of the adventure, he called on Madame d'Estillac, an old gambler, whose house is open till four in the morning; that everybody there was surprised at the disordered state in which he appeared; that his bagwig had fallen off, one skirt of his coat was cut, and his right hand bleeding. That they instantly bound it up, and gave him some Rota wine. Four days ago, the Duc de C— — supped with the King, and sat near M. de St. Florentin. He talked to him of his relation's adventure, and asked him if he had made any inquiries concerning the lady. M. de St. Florentin coldly answered, 'No!' and M. de C— — remarked, on asking him some further questions, that he kept his eyes firmed on his plate, looking embarrassed, and answered in monosyllables. He asked him the reason of this, upon which M. de Florentin told him that it was extremely distressing to him to see him under such a mistake. 'How can you know that, supposing it to be the fact?' said M. de — — —, 'Nothing is more easy to prove,' replied M. de St. Florentin. 'You may imagine that, as soon as I was informed of the Marquis de — — —'s adventure, I set on foot inquiries, the result of which was, that, on the night when this affair was said to have taken place, a party of the watch was set in ambuscade in this very street, for the purpose of catching a thief who was coming out of the gaming house; that this party was there four hours, and heard not the slightest noise.' M. de C was greatly incensed at this recital, which M. de St. Florentin ought, indeed, to have communicated to the King. He has ordered, or will order, his relation to retire to his province.

"After this, you will judge, my dear, whether you were very likely to be graciously received when you went open-mouthed with your compliment to the Marquise. This adventure," continued she, "reminded the King of one which occurred about fifteen years ago. The

Comte d'E— —, who was what is called 'enfant d'honneur' to the Dauphin, and about fourteen years of age, came into the Dauphin's apartments, one evening, with his bag-wig snatched off, and his ruffles torn, and said that, having walked rather late near the piece of water des Suisses, he had been attacked by two robbers; that he had refused to give them anything, drawn his sword, and put himself in an attitude of defence; that one of the robbers was armed with a sword, the other with a large stick, from which he had received several blows, but that he had wounded one in the arm, and that, hearing a noise at that moment, they had fled. But unluckily for the little Count, it was known that people were on the spot at the precise time he mentioned, and had heard nothing. The Count was pardoned, on account of his youth. The Dauphin made him confess the truth, and it was looked upon as a childish freak to set people talking about him."

The King disliked the King of Prussia because he knew that the latter was in the habit of jesting upon his mistress, and the kind of life he led. It was Frederick's fault, as I have heard it said, that the King was not his most steadfast ally and friend, as much as sovereigns can be towards each other; but the jestings of Frederick had stung him, and made him conclude the treaty of Versailles. One day, he entered Madame's apartment with a paper in his hand, and said, "The King of Prussia is certainly a great man; he loves men of talent, and, like Louis XIV., he wishes to make Europe ring with his favours towards foreign savans. There is a letter from him, addressed to Milord Marshal,

[George Keith, better known under the name of Milord Marshal, was the eldest son of William Keith, Earl Marshal of Scotland. He was an avowed partisan of the Stuarts, and did not lay down the arms he had taken up in their cause until it became utterly desperate, and drew upon its defenders useless dangers. When they were driven from their country, he renounced it, and took up his residence successively in France, Prussia, Spain, and Italy. The delicious country and climate of Valencia he preferred above any other.

Milord Marshal died in the month of May, 1778. It was he who said to Madame Geoffrin, speaking of his brother, who was field-marshal in the Prussian service, and died on the field of honour,

"My brother leaves me the most glorious inheritance" (he had just laid the whole of Bohemia under contribution); "his property does not amount to seventy ducats." A eulogium on Milord Marshal, by D'Alembert, is extant. It is the most cruelly mangled of all his works, by Linguet]

ordering him to acquaint a 'superieur' man of my kingdom (D'Alembert) that he has granted him a "pension;" and, looking at the letter, he read the following words: "You must know that there is in Paris a man of the greatest merit, whose fortune is not proportionate to his talents and character. I may serve as eyes to the blind goddess, and repair in some measure the injustice, and I beg you to offer on that account. I flatter myself that he will accept this pension because of the pleasure I shall feel in obliging a man who joins beauty of character to the most sublime intellectual talents." The King here stopped, on seeing MM. de Ayen and de Gontaut enter, and then recommenced reading the letter to them, and added, "It was given me by the Minister for Foreign Affairs, to whom it was confided by Milord Marshal, for the purpose of obtaining my permission for this sublime genius to accept the favour. But," said the King, "what do you think is the amount?" Some said six, eight, ten thousand livres. "You have not guessed," said the King; "it is twelve hundred livres."—"For sublime talents," said the Duc d'Ayen, "it is not much. But the philosophers will make Europe resound with this letter, and the King of Prussia will have the pleasure of making a great noise at little expense."

The Chevalier de Courten,—[The Chevalier de Courten was a Swiss, and a man of talent.]—who had been in Prussia, came in, and, hearing this story told, said, "I have seen what is much better than that: passing through a village in Prussia, I got out at the posthouse, while I was waiting for horses; and the postmaster, who was a captain in the Prussian service, showed me several letters in Frederick's handwriting, addressed to his uncle, who was a man of rank, promising him to provide for his nephews; the provision he made for this, the eldest of these nephews, who was dreadfully wounded, was the postmastership which he then held." M. de Marigny related this story at Quesnay's, and added, that the man of genius above mentioned was D'Alembert, and that the King had permitted him to accept the pension. He added, that his sister had suggested to the

King that he had better give D'Alembert a pension of twice the value, and forbid him to take the King of Prussia's. This advice he would not take, because he looked upon D'Alembert as an infidel. M. de Marigny took a copy of the letter, which he lent me.

A certain nobleman, at one time, affected to cast tender glances on Madame Adelaide. She was wholly unconscious of it; but, as there are Arguses at Court, the King was, of course, told of it, and, indeed, he thought he had perceived it himself. I know that he came into Madame de Pompadour's room one day, in a great passion, and said, "Would you believe that there is a man in my Court insolent enough to dare to raise his eyes to one of my daughters?" Madame had never seen him so exasperated, and this illustrious nobleman was advised to feign a necessity for visiting his estates. He remained there two months. Madame told me, long after, that she thought that there were no tortures to which the King would not have condemned any man who had seduced one of his daughters. Madame Adelaide, at the time in question, was a charming person, and united infinite grace, and much talent, to a most agreeable face.

A courier brought Madame de Pompadour a letter, on reading which she burst into tears. It contained the intelligence of the battle of Rosbach, which M. de Soubise sent her, with all the details. I heard her say to the Marechal de Belle-Isle, wiping her eyes, "M. de Soubise is inconsolable; he does not try to excuse his conduct, he sees nothing but the disastrous fortune which pursues him."—"M. de Soubise must, however, have many things to urge in his own behalf," said M. de Belle-Isle, "and so I told the King."—"It is very noble in you, Marshal, not to suffer an unfortunate man to be overwhelmed; the public are furious against him, and what has he done to deserve it?"—"There is not a more honourable nor a kinder man in the world. I only fulfil my duty in doing justice to the truth, and to a man for whom I have the most profound esteem. The King will explain to you, Madame, how M. de Soubise was forced to give battle by the Prince of Sage-Hildbourgshausen, whose troops fled first, and carried along the French troops." Madame would have embraced the old Marshal if she had dared, she was so delighted with him.

M. de Soubise, having gained a battle, was made Marshal of France: Madame was enchanted with her friend's success. But, either it was unimportant, or the public were offended at his promotion; nobody talked of it but Madame's friends. This unpopularity was concealed from her, and she said to Colin, her steward, at her toilet, "Are you not delighted at the victory M. de Soubise has gained? What does the public say of it? He has taken his revenge well." Colin was embarrassed, and knew not what to answer. As she pressed him further, he replied that he had been ill, and had seen nobody for a week.

M. de Marigny came to see me one day, very much out of humour. I asked him the cause. "I have," said he, "just been intreating my sister not to make M. le Normand-de-Mezi Minister of the Marine. I told her that she was heaping coals of fire upon her own head. A favourite ought not to multiply the points of attack upon herself." The Doctor entered. "You," said the Doctor, "are worth your weight in gold, for the good sense and capacity you have shewn in your office, and for your moderation, but you will never be appreciated as you deserve; your advice is excellent; there will never be a ship taken but Madame will be held responsible for it to the public, and you are very wise not to think of being in the Ministry yourself."

One day, when I was at Paris, I went to dine with the Doctor, who happened to be there at the same time; there were, contrary to his usual custom, a good many people, and, among others, a handsome young Master of the Requests, who took a title from some place, the name of which I have forgotten, but who was a son of M. Turgot, the 'prevot des marchands'. They talked a great deal about administration, which was not very amusing to me; they then fell upon the subject of the love Frenchmen bear to their Kings. M. Turgot here joined in the conversation, and said, "This is not a blind attachment; it is a deeply rooted sentiment, arising from an indistinct recollection of great benefits. The French nation—I may go farther— Europe, and all mankind, owe to a King of France" (I have forgotten his name)—[Phillip the Long]—"whatever liberty they enjoy. He established communes, and conferred on an immense number of men a civil existence. I am aware that it may be said, with justice, that he served his own interests by granting these franchises; that the cities paid him taxes, and that his design was to use them as instruments of weakening the power of great nobles; but what does that prove, but that this measure was at once useful, politic, and humane?" From Kings in general the conversation turned upon Louis XV., and M. Turgot remarked that his reign would be always celebrated for the advancement of the sciences, the progress of knowledge, and of philosophy. He added that Louis XV. was deficient in the quality which Louis XIV. possessed to excess; that is to say, in a good opinion of himself; that he was well-informed; that nobody was more perfectly master of the topography of France; that his opinion in the Council was always the most judicious; and that it was much to be lamented that he had not more confidence in himself, or that he did not rely upon some Minister who enjoyed the confidence of the nation. Everybody agreed with him. I begged M. Quesnay to write down what young Turgot had said, and showed it to Madame. She praised this Master of the Requests greatly, and spoke of him to the King. "It is a good breed," said he.

One day, I went out to walk, and saw, on my return, a great many people going and coming, and speaking to each other privately: it was evident that something extraordinary had happened. I asked a person of my acquaintance what was the matter. "Alas!" said he, with tears in his eyes, "some assassins, who had formed the project of murdering the King, have inflicted several wounds on a garde-du-corps, who overheard them in a dark corridor; he is carried to the hospital: and as he has described the colour of these men's coats, the Police are in quest of them in all directions, and some people, dressed in clothes of that colour, are already arrested." I saw Madame with M. de Gontaut, and I hastened home. She found her door besieged by a multitude of people, and was alarmed: when she got in, she found the Comte de Noailles. "What is all this, Count?" said she. He said he was come expressly to speak to her, and they retired to her closet together. The conference was not long. I had remained in the drawing-room, with Madame's equerry, the Chevalier de Solent, Gourbillon, her valet de chambre, and some strangers. A great many details were related; but, the wounds being little more than scratches, and the garde-du-corps having let fall some contradictions, it was thought that he was an impostor, who had invented all this story to bring himself into favour. Before the night was over, this was proved to be the fact, and, I believe, from his own confession. The King came, that evening, to see Madame de Pompadour; he spoke of this occurrence with great sang froid, and said, "The gentleman who wanted to kill me was a wicked madman; this is a low scoundrel."

When he spoke of Damiens, which was only while his trial lasted, he never called him anything but that gentleman.

I have heard it said that he proposed having him shut up in a dungeon for life; but that the horrible nature of the crime made the judges insist upon his suffering all the tortures inflicted upon like occasions. Great numbers, many of them women, had a barbarous curiosity to witness the execution; amongst others, Madame de P— ——, a very beautiful woman, and the wife of a Farmer General. She hired two places at a window for twelve Louis, and played a game of cards in the room whilst waiting for the execution to begin. On this being told to the King, he covered his eyes with his hands and exclaimed, "Fi, la Vilaine!" I have been told that she, and others, thought to pay their court in this way, and signalise their attachment to the King's person.

Two things were related to me by M. Duclos at the time of the attempt on the King's life.

The first, relative to the Comte de Sponheim, who was the Duc de Deux-Ponts, and next in succession to the Palatinate and Electorate of Bavaria. He was thought to be a great friend to the King, and had made several long sojourns in France. He came frequently to see Madame. M. Duclos told us that the Duc de Deux-Ponts, having learned, at Deux-Ponts, the attempt on the King's life, immediately set out in a carriage for Versailles: "But remark," said he, "the spirit of 'courtisanerie' of a Prince, who may be Elector of Bavaria and the Palatinate tomorrow. This was not enough. When he arrived within ten leagues of Paris, he put on an enormous pair of jack-boots, mounted a post-horse, and arrived in the court of the palace cracking his whip. If this had been real impatience, and not charlatanism, he would have taken horse twenty leagues from Paris."—"I don't agree with you," said a gentleman whom I did not know; "impatience sometimes seizes one towards the end of an undertaking, and one employs the readiest means then in one's power. Besides, the Duc de Deux-Ponts might wish, by showing himself thus on horseback, to serve the King, to whom he is attached, by proving to Frenchmen how greatly he is beloved and honoured in other countries." Duclos resumed: "Well," said he, "do you know the story of M. de C———? The first day the King saw company, after the attempt of Damiens, M. de C——- pushed so vigorously through the crowd that he was one of the first to come into the King's presence, but he had on so shabby a black coat that it caught the King's attention, who burst out laughing, and said, 'Look at C———-, he has had the skirt of his coat torn off.' M. de C——- looked as if he was only then first conscious of his loss, and said, 'Sire, there is such a multitude hurrying to see Your Majesty, that I was obliged to fight my way through them, and, in the effort, my coat has been torn.'—'Fortunately it was not worth much,' said the Marquis de Souvre, 'and you could not have chosen a worse one to sacrifice on the occasion.'"

Madame de Pompadour had been very judiciously advised to get her husband, M. le Normand, sent to Constantinople, as Ambassador. This would have a little diminished the scandal caused by seeing Madame de Pompadour, with the title of Marquise, at Court, and her husband Farmer General at Paris. But he was so attached to a Paris life, and to his opera habits, that he could not be prevailed upon to go. Madame employed a certain M. d'Arboulin, with whom she had been acquainted before she was at Court, to negotiate this affair. He applied to a Mademoiselle Rem, who had been an opera-dancer, and who was M. le Normand's mistress. She made him very fine promises; but she was like him, and preferred a Paris life. She would do nothing in it.

At the time that plays were acted in the little apartments, I obtained a lieutenancy for one of my relations, by a singular means, which proves the value the greatest people set upon the slightest access to the Court. Madame did not like to ask anything of M. d'Argenson, and, being pressed by my family, who could not imagine that, situated as I was, it could be difficult for me to obtain a command for a good soldier, I determined to go and ask the Comte d'Argenson. I made my request, and presented my memorial. He received me coldly, and gave me vague answers. I went out, and the Marquis de V— —-, who was in his closet, followed me. "You wish to obtain a command," said he; "there is one vacant, which is promised me for one of my proteges; but if you will do me a favour in return, or obtain one for me, I will give it to you. I want to be a police officer, and you have it in your power to get me a place." I told him I did not understand the purport of his jest. "I will tell you," said he; "Tartuffe is going to be acted in the cabinets, and there is the part of a police officer, which only consists of a few lines. Prevail upon Madame de Pompadour to assign me that part, and the command is yours." I promised nothing, but I related the history to Madame, who said she would arrange it for me. The thing was done, and I obtained the command, and the Marquis de V— —- thanked Madame as if she had made him a Duke.

The King was often annoyed by the Parliaments, and said a very remarkable thing concerning them, which M. de Gontaut repeated to Doctor Quesnay in my presence. "Yesterday," said he, "the King walked up and down the room with an anxious air. Madame de Pompadour asked him if he was uneasy about his health, as he had been, for some time, rather unwell. 'No,' replied he; 'but I am greatly annoyed by all these remonstrances.'—'What can come of them,' said she, 'that need seriously disquiet Your Majesty? Are you not master of the Parliaments, as well as of all the rest of the kingdom?'—'That is true,' said the King; 'but, if it had not been for these counsellors and presidents, I should never have been stabbed by that gentleman' (he always called Damiens so). 'Ah! Sire,' cried Madame de Pompadour. 'Read the trial,' said he. 'It was the language of those gentlemen he names which turned his head.'—'But,' said Madame, 'I have often thought that, if the Archbishop—[M. de Beaumont]—could be sent to Rome—'—'Find anybody who will accomplish that business, and I will give him whatever he pleases.'" Quesnay said the King was right in all he had uttered. The Archbishop was exiled shortly after, and the King was seriously afflicted at being driven to take such a step. "What a pity," he often said, "that so excellent a man should be so obstinate."—"And so shallow," said somebody, one day. "Hold your tongue," replied the King, somewhat sternly. The Archbishop was very charitable, and liberal to excess, but he often granted pensions without discernment.

[The following is a specimen of the advantages taken of his natural kindness. Madame la Caille, who acted the Duennas at the Opera Comique, was recommended to him as the mother of a family, who deserved his protection, The worthy prelate asked what he could do for her. Monseigneur," said the actress, "two words from your hand to the Duc de Richelieu would induce him to grant me a demi-part." M. de Beaumont, who was very little acquainted with the language of the theatre, thought that a demi-part meant a more liberal portion of the Marshal's alms, and the note was written in the most pressing manner. The Marshal answered, that he thanked the Archbishop for the interest he took in the Theatre Italien, and in Madame la Caille, who was a very useful person at that theatre; that, nevertheless, she had a bad voice; but that the recommendation of the Archbishop was to be preferred to the greatest talents, and that the demi-part was granted."]

He granted one of an hundred louis to a pretty woman, who was very poor, and who assumed an illustrious name, to which she had no right. The fear lest she should be plunged into vice led him to bestow such excessive bounty upon her; and the woman was an admirable dissembler. She went to the Archbishop's, covered with a great hood, and, when she left him, she amused herself with a variety of lovers.

Great people have the bad habit of talking very indiscreetly before their servants. M. de Gontaut once said these words, covertly, as he thought, to the Duc de — — —, "That measures had been taken which would, probably, have the effect of determining the Archbishop to go to Rome, with a Cardinal's hat; and that, if he desired it, he was to have a coadjutor."

A very plausible pretext had been found for making this proposition, and for rendering it flattering to the Archbishop, and agreeable to his sentiments. The affair had been very adroitly begun, and success appeared certain. The King had the air, towards the Archbishop, of entire unconsciousness of what was going on. The negotiator acted as if he were only following the suggestions of his own mind, for the general good. He was a friend of the Archbishop, and was very sure of a liberal reward. A valet of the Duc de Gontaut, a very handsome young fellow, had perfectly caught the sense of what was spoken in a mysterious manner. He was one of the lovers of the lady of the hundred Louis a year, and had heard her talk of the Archbishop, whose relation she pretended to be. He thought he should secure her good graces by informing her that great efforts were being made to induce her patron to reside at Rome, with a view to get him away from Paris. The lady instantly told the Archbishop, as she was afraid of losing her pension if he went. The information squared so well with the negotiation then on foot, that the Archbishop had no doubt of its truth. He cooled, by degrees, in his conversations with the negotiator, whom he regarded as a traitor, and ended by breaking with him. These details were not known till long afterwards. The lover of the lady having been sent to the Bicetre, some letters were found among his papers, which gave a scent of the affair, and he was made to confess the rest.

In order not to compromise the Duc de Gontaut, the King was told that the valet had come to a knowledge of the business from a letter which he had found in his master's clothes. The King took his revenge by humiliating the Archbishop, which he was enabled to do by means of the information he had obtained concerning the conduct of the lady, his protege. She was found guilty of swindling, in concert with her beloved valet; but, before her punishment was inflicted, the Lieutenant of Police was ordered to lay before Monseigneur a full account of the conduct of his relation and pensioner. The Archbishop had nothing to object to in the proofs which were submitted to him; he said, with perfect calmness, that she was not his relation; and, raising his hands to heaven, "She is an unhappy wretch," said he, "who has robbed me of the money which was destined for the poor. But God knows that, in giving her so large a pension, I did not act lightly. I had, at that time, before my eyes the example of a young woman who once asked me to grant her seventy louis a year, promising me that she would always live very virtuously, as she had hitherto done. I refused her, and she said, on leaving me, 'I must turn to the left, Monseigneur, since the way on the right is closed against me: The unhappy creature has kept her word but too well. She found means of establishing a faro-table at her house, which is tolerated; and she joins to the most profligate conduct in her own person the infamous trade of a corrupter of youth; her house is the abode of every vice. Think, sir, after that, whether it was not an act of prudence, on my part, to grant the woman in question a pension, suitable to the rank in which I thought her born, to prevent her abusing the gifts of youth, beauty, and talents, which she possessed, to her own perdition, and the destruction of others." The Lieutenant of Police told the King that he was touched with the candour and the noble simplicity of the prelate. "I never doubted his virtues," replied the King, "but I wish he would be quiet." This same Archbishop gave a pension of fifty louis a year to the greatest scoundrel in Paris. He is a poet, who writes abominable verses; this pension is granted on condition that his poems are never printed. I learned this fact from M. de Marigny, to whom he recited some of his horrible verses one evening, when he supped with him, in company with some people of quality. He chinked the money in his pocket. "This is my good Archbishop's," said he, laughing; "I keep my word with him: my poem will not be printed during my life, but I read it. What would the good prelate say if he knew that I shared my last quarter's allowance with a charming little opera-dancer? 'It is the Archbishop, then, who keeps me,' said she to me; 'Oh, la! how droll that is!'" The King heard this, and was much scandalised at it. "How difficult it is to do good!" said he.

The King came into Madame de Pompadour's room, one day, as she was finishing dressing. "I have just had a strange adventure," said he: "would you believe that, in going out of my wardroom into my bedroom, I met a gentleman face to face?" — "My God! Sire," cried Madame, terrified. "It was nothing," replied he; "but I confess I was greatly surprised: the man appeared speechless with consternation. 'What do you do here?' said I, civilly. He threw himself on his knees, saying, 'Pardon me, Sire; and, above all, have me searched: He instantly emptied his pockets himself; he pulled off his coat in the greatest agitation and terror: at last he told me that he was cook to — —-, and a friend of Beccari, whom he came to visit; that he had mistaken the staircase, and, finding all the doors open, he had wandered into the room in which I found him, and which he would have instantly left: I rang; Guimard came, and was astonished enough at finding me tete-a-tete with a man in his shirt. He begged Guimard to go with him into another room, and to search his whole person. After this, the poor devil returned, and put on his coat. Guimard said to me, 'He is certainly an honest man, and tells the truth; this may, besides, be easily ascertained.' Another of the servants of the palace came in, and happened to know him. 'I will answer for this good man,' said, he, 'who, moreover, makes the best 'boeuf a carlate' in the world.' As I saw the man was so agitated that he could not stand steady, I took fifty louis out of my bureau, and said, Here, sir, are fifty Louis, to quiet your alarms: He went out, after throwing himself at my feet." Madame exclaimed on the impropriety of having the King's bedroom thus accessible to everybody. He talked with great calmness of this strange apparition, but it was evident that he controlled himself, and that he had, in fact, been much frightened, as, indeed, he had reason to be. Madame highly approved of the gift; and she was the more right in applauding it, as it was by no means in the King's usual manner. M. de Marigny said, when I told him of this adventure, that he would have wagered a thousand louis against the King's making a present of fifty, if anybody but I had told him of the circumstance. "It is a singular fact," continued he, "that all of the race of Valois have been liberal to excess; this is not precisely the case with the Bourbons, who are rather reproached with avarice. Henri IV. was said to be avaricious. He gave to his mistresses, because he could refuse them nothing; but he played with the eagerness of a man whose whole fortune depends on the game. Louis XIV. gave through ostentation. It is most astonishing," added he, "to reflect on what might have happened. The King might actually have been assassinated in his chamber, without anybody knowing anything of the matter and without a possibility of discovering the murderer." For more than a fortnight Madame could not get over this incident.

About that time she had a quarrel with her brother, and both were in the right. Proposals were made to him to marry the daughter of one of the greatest noblemen of the Court, and the King consented to create him a Duke, and even to make the title hereditary. Madame was right in wishing to aggrandise her brother, but he declared that he valued his liberty above all things, and that he would not sacrifice it except for a person he really loved. He was a true Epicurean philosopher, and a man of great capacity, according to the report of those who knew him well, and judged him impartially. It was entirely at his option to have had the reversion of M. de St. Florentin's place, and the place of Minister of Marine, when M. de Machault retired; he said to his sister, at the time, "I spare you many vexations, by depriving you of a slight satisfaction. The people would be unjust to me, however well I might fulfil the duties of my office. As to M. de St. Florentin's place, he may live five-and-twenty years, so that I should not be the better for it. Kings' mistresses are hated enough on their own account; they need not also draw upon, themselves the hatred which is directed against Ministers." M. Quesnay repeated this conversation to me.

The King had another mistress, who gave Madame de Pompadour some uneasiness. She was a woman of quality, and the wife of one of the most assiduous courtiers.

A man in immediate attendance on the King's person, and who had the care of his clothes, came to me one day, and told me that, as he was very much attached to Madame, because she was good and useful to the King, he wished to inform me that, a letter having fallen out of the pocket of a coat which His Majesty had taken off, he had had the curiosity to read it, and found it to be from the Comtesse de — —- who had already yielded to the King's desires. In this letter, she required the King to give her fifty thousand crowns in money, a regiment for one of her relations, and a bishopric for another, and to dismiss Madame in the space of fifteen days, etc. I acquainted Madame with what this man told me, and she acted with singular greatness of mind. She said to me, "I ought to inform the King of this breach of trust of his servant, who may, by the same means, come to the knowledge of, and make a bad use of, important secrets; but I feel a repugnance to ruin the man: however, I cannot permit him to remain near the King's person, and here is what I shall do: Tell him that there is a place of ten thousand francs a year vacant in one of the provinces; let him solicit the Minister of Finance for it, and it shall be granted to him; but, if he should ever disclose through what interest he has obtained it, the King shall be made acquainted with his conduct. By this means, I think I shall have done all that my attachment and duty prescribe. I rid the King of a faithless domestic, without ruining the individual." I did as Madame ordered me: her delicacy and address inspired me with admiration. She was not alarmed on account of the lady, seeing what her pretentions were. "She drives too quick," remarked Madame, "and will certainly be overturned on the road." The lady died.

"See what the Court is; all is corruption there, from the highest to the lowest," said I to Madame, one day, when she was speaking to me of some facts, that had come to my knowledge. "I could tell you many others," replied Madame; "but the little chamber, where you often remain, must furnish you with a sufficient number." This was a little nook, from, whence I could hear a great part of what passed in Madame's apartment. The Lieutenant of Police sometimes came secretly to this apartment, and waited there. Three or four persons, of high consideration, also found their way in, in a mysterious, manner, and several devotees, who were, in their hearts, enemies of Madame de Pompadour. But these men had not petty objects in view: one: required the government of a province; another, a seat in the Council; a third, a Captaincy of the, Guards; and this man would have obtained it if the Marechale de Mirepoix had not requested it for her brother, the Prince de Beauvan. The Chevalier du Muy was not among these apostates; not even the promise of being High Constable would have tempted him to make up to Madame, still less to betray his master, the Dauphin. This Prince was, to the last degree, weary of the station he held. Sometimes, when teased to death by ambitious people, who pretended to be Catos, or wonderfully devout, he took part against a Minister against whom he was prepossessed; then relapsed into his accustomed state of inactivity and ennui.

The King used to say, "My son is lazy; his temper is Polonese — hasty and changeable; he has no tastes; he cares nothing for hunting, for women, or for good living; perhaps he imagines that if he were in my place he would be happy; at first, he would make great changes, create everything anew, as it were. In a short time he would be as tired of the rank of King as he now is of his own; he is only fit to live 'en philosophe', with clever people about him." The King added, "He loves what is right; he is truly virtuous, and does not want under standing."

M. de St. Germain said, one day, to the King, "To think well of mankind, one must be neither a Confessor, nor a Minister, nor a Lieutenant of Police." — "Nor a King," said His Majesty. "Ah! Sire," replied he, "you remember the fog we had a few days ago, when we could not see four steps before us. Kings are commonly surrounded by still thicker fogs, collected around them by men of intriguing character, and faithless Ministers—all, of every class, unite in endeavouring to make things appear to Kings in any, light but the true one." I heard this from the mouth of the famous Comte de St. Germain, as I was attending upon Madame, who was ill in bed. The King was there; and the Count, who was a welcome visitor, had been admitted. There were also present, M. de Gontaut, Madame de Brancas, and the Abbe de Bernis. I remember that the very same day, after the Count was gone out, the King talked in a style which gave Madame great pain. Speaking of the King of Prussia, he said, "That is a madman, who will risk all to gain all, and may, perhaps, win the game, though he has neither religion, morals, nor principles. He wants to make a noise in the world, and he will succeed. Julian, the Apostate, did the same."—"I never saw the King so animated before," observed Madame, when he was gone out; "and really the comparison with Julian, the Apostate, is not amiss, considering the irreligion of the King of Prussia. If he gets out of his perplexities, surrounded as he is by his enemies, he will be one of the greatest men in history."

M. de Bernis remarked, "Madame is correct in her judgment, for she has no reason to pronounce his praises; nor have I, though I agree with what she says." Madame de Pompadour never enjoyed so much influence as at the time when M. de Choiseul became one of the Ministry. From the time of the Abbe de Bernis she had afforded him her constant support, and he had been employed in foreign affairs, of which he was said to know but little. Madame made the Treaty of Sienna, though the first idea of it was certainly furnished her by the Abbe. I have been informed by several persons that the King often talked to Madame upon this subject; for my own part, I never heard any conversation relative to it, except the high praises bestowed by her on the Empress and the Prince de Kaunitz, whom she had known a good deal of. She said that he had a clear head, the head of a statesman. One day, when she was talking in this strain, some one tried to cast ridicule upon the Prince on account of the style in which he wore his hair, and the four valets de chambre, who made the hair-powder fly in all directions, while Kaunitz ran about that he might only catch the superfine part of it. "Aye," said Madame, "just as Alcibiades cut off his dog's tail in order to give the Athenians something to talk about, and to turn their attention from those things he wished to conceal."

Never was the public mind so inflamed against Madame de Pompadour as when news arrived of the battle of Rosbach. Every day she received anonymous letters, full of the grossest abuse; atrocious verses, threats of poison and assassination. She continued long a prey to the most acute sorrow, and could get no sleep but from opiates. All this discontent was excited by her protecting the Prince of Soubise; and the Lieutenant of Police had great difficulty in allaying the ferment of the people. The King affirmed that it was not his fault. M. du Verney was the confidant of Madame in everything relating to war; a subject which he well understood, though not a military man by, profession. The old Marechal de Noailles called him, in derision, the General of the flour, but Marechal Saxe, one day, told Madame that Du Verney knew more of military matters than the old Marshal. Du Verney once paid a visit to Madame de Pompadour, and found her in company with the King, the Minister of War, and two Marshals; he submitted to them the plan of a campaign, which was generally applauded. It was through his influence that M. de Richelieu was appointed to the command of the army, instead of the Marechal d'Estrdes. He came to Quesnay two days after, when I was with him. The Doctor began talking about the art of war, and I remember he said, "Military men make a great mystery of their art; but what is the reason that young Princes have always the most brilliant success? Why, because they are active and daring. When Sovereigns command their troops in person what exploits they perform! Clearly, because they are at liberty to run all risks." These observations made a lasting impression on my mind.

The first physician came, one day, to see Madame he was talking of madmen and madness. The King was present, and everything relating to disease of any kind interested him. The first physician said that he could distinguish the symptoms of approaching madness six months beforehand. "Are there any persons about the Court likely to become mad?" said the King.—"I know one who will be imbecile in less than three months," replied he. The King pressed him to tell the name. He excused himself for some time. At last he said, "It is M. de Sechelles, the Controller-General." — "You have a spite against him," said Madame, "because he would not grant what you asked" — "That is true," said he, "but though that might possibly incline me to tell a disagreeable truth, it would not make me invent one. He is losing his intellects from debility. He affects gallantry at his age, and I perceive the connection in his ideas is becoming feeble and irregular." — The King laughed; but three months afterwards he came to Madame, saying, "Sechelles gives evident proofs of dotage in the Council. We must appoint a successor to him." Madame de Pompadour told me of this on the way to Choisy. Some time afterwards, the first physician came to see Madame, and spoke to her in private. "You are attached to M. Berryer, Madame," said he, "and I am sorry to have to warn you that he will be attacked by madness, or by catalepsy, before long. I saw him this morning at chapel, sitting on one of those very low little chairs, which are only, meant to kneel upon. His knees touched his chin. I went to his house after Mass; his eyes were wild, and when his secretary spoke to him, he said, 'Hold your tongue, pen. A pen's business is to write, and not to speak.'" Madame, who liked the Keeper of the Seals, was very much concerned, and begged the first physician not to mention what he had perceived. Four days after this, M. Berryer was seized with catalepsy, after having talked incoherently. This is a disease which I did not know even by name, and got it written down for me. The patient remains in precisely the same position in which the fit seizes him; one leg or arm elevated, the eyes wide open, or just as it may happen. This latter affair was known to all the Court at the death of the Keeper of the Seals.

When the Marechal de Belle-Isle's son was killed in battle, Madame persuaded the King to pay his father a visit. He was rather reluctant, and Madame said to him, with an air half angry, half playful:

————"Barbare! don't l'orgueil
Croit le sang d'un sujet trop pays d'un coup d'oeil."

The King laughed, and said, "Whose fine verses are those?" — "Voltaire's," said Madame ———.

"As barbarous as I am, I gave him the place of gentleman in ordinary, and a pension," said the King.

The King went in state to call on the Marshal, followed by all the Court; and it certainly appeared that this solemn visit consoled the Marshal for the loss of his son, the sole heir to his name.

When the Marshal died, he was carried to his house on a common hand-barrow, covered with a shabby cloth. I met the body. The bearers were laughing and singing. I thought it was some servant, and asked who it was. How great was my surprise at learning that these were the remains of a man abounding in honours and in riches. Such is the Court; the dead are always in fault, and cannot be put out of sight too soon.

The King said, "M. Fouquet is dead, I hear." — "He was no longer Fouquet," replied the Duc d'Ayen; "Your Majesty had permitted him to change that name, under which, however, he acquired all his reputation." The King shrugged his shoulders. His Majesty had, in fact, granted him letters patent, permitting him not to sign Fouquet during his Ministry. I heard this on the occasion in question. M. de Choiseul had the war department at his death. He was every day more and more in favour.

Madame treated him with greater distinction than any previous Minister, and his manners towards her were the most agreeable it is possible to conceive, at once respectful and gallant. He never passed a day without seeing her. M. de Marigny could not endure M. de Choiseul, but he never spoke of him, except to his intimate friends. Calling, one day, at Quesnay's, I found him there. They were talking of M. de Choiseul. "He is a mere 'petit maitre'," said the Doctor, "and, if he were handsome just fit to be one of Henri the Third's favourites." The Marquis de Mirabeau and M. de La Riviere came in. "This kingdom," said Mirabeau, "is in a deplorable state. There is neither national energy, nor the only substitute for it — money." — "It can only be regenerated," said La Riviere, "by a conquest, like that of China, or by some great internal convulsion; but woe to those who live to see that! The French people do not do things by halves." These words made me tremble, and I hastened out of the room. M. de Marigny did the same, though without appearing at all affected by what had been said. "You heard De La Riviere," said he, — "but don't be alarmed, the conversations that pass at the Doctor's are never repeated; these are honourable men, though rather chimerical. They know not where to stop. I think, however, they are in the right way; only, unfortunately, they go too far." I wrote this down immediately.

The Comte de St. Germain came to see Madame de Pompadour, who was ill, and lay on the sofa. He shewed her a little box, containing topazes, rubies, and emeralds. He appeared to have enough to furnish a treasury. Madame sent for me to see all these beautiful things. I looked at them with an air of the utmost astonishment, but I made signs to Madame that I thought them all false. The Count felt for something in his pocketbook, about twice as large as a spectacle-case, and, at length, drew out two or three little paper packets, which he unfolded, and exhibited a superb ruby. He threw on the table, with a contemptuous air, a little cross of green and white stones. I looked at it and said, "That is not to be despised." I put it on, and admired it greatly. The Count begged me to accept it. I refused—he urged me to take it. Madame then refused it for me. At length, he pressed it upon me so warmly that Madame, seeing that it could not be worth above forty Louis, made me a sign to accept it. I took the cross, much pleased at the Count's politeness; and, some days after, Madame presented him with an enamelled box, upon which was the portrait of some Grecian sage (whose name I don't recollect), to whom she compared him. I skewed the cross to a jeweller, who valued it at sixty-five Louis. The Count offered to bring Madame some enamel portraits, by Petitot, to look at, and she told him to bring them after dinner, while the King was hunting. He shewed his portraits, after which Madame said to him, "I have heard a great deal of a charming story you told two days ago, at supper, at M. le Premier's, of an occurrence you witnessed fifty or sixty years ago." He smiled and said, "It is rather long."—"So much the better," said she, with an air of delight. Madame de Gontaut and the ladies came in, and the door was shut; Madame made a sign to me to sit down behind the screen. The Count made many apologies for the ennui which his story would, perhaps, occasion. He said, "Sometimes one can tell a story pretty well; at other times it is quite a different thing."

"At the beginning of this century, the Marquis de St. Gilles was Ambassador from Spain to the Hague. In his youth he had been particularly intimate with the Count of Moncade, a grandee of Spain, and one of the richest nobles of that country. Some months after the Marquis's arrival at the Hague, he received a letter from the Count, entreating him, in the name of their former friendship, to render him the greatest possible service. 'You know,' said he, 'my dear Marquis, the mortification I felt that the name of Moncade was likely to expire with me. At length, it pleased heaven to hear my prayers, and to grant me a son: he gave early promise of dispositions worthy of his birth, but he, some time since, formed an unfortunate and disgraceful attachment to the most celebrated actress of the company of Toledo. I shut my eyes to this imprudence on the part of a young man whose conduct had, till then, caused me unmingled satisfaction. But, having learnt that he was so blinded by passion as to intend to marry this girl, and that he had even bound himself by a written promise to that effect, I solicited the King to have her placed in confinement. My son, having got information of the steps I had taken, defeated my intentions by escaping with the object of his passion. For more than six months I have vainly endeavoured to discover where he has concealed himself, but I have now some reason to think he is at the Hague. The Count earnestly conjured the Marquis to make the most rigid search, in order to discover his son's retreat, and to endeavour to prevail upon him to return to his home. 'It is an act of justice,' continued he, 'to provide for the, girl, if she consents to give up the written promise of marriage which she has received, and I leave it to your discretion to do what is right for her, as well as to determine the sum necessary to bring my son to Madrid in a manner suitable to his condition. I know not,' concluded he, 'whether you are a father; if you are, you will be able to sympathise in my anxieties.' The Count subjoined to this letter an exact description of his son, and the young woman by whom he was accompanied.

"On the receipt of this letter, the Marquis lost not a moment in sending to all the inns in Amsterdam, Rotterdam, and the Hague, but in vain—he could find no trace of them. He began to despair of success, when the idea struck him that a young French page of his, remarkable for his quickness and intelligence, might be employed with advantage. He promised to reward him handsomely if he succeeded in finding the young woman, who was the cause of so much anxiety, and gave him the description of her person. The page visited all the public places for many days, without success; at length, one evening, at the play, he saw a young man and woman, in a box, who attracted his attention. When he saw that they, perceived he was looking at them, and withdrew to the back of the box to avoid his observation, he felt confident that they were the objects of his search. He did not take his eyes from the bog, and watched every movement in it. The instant the performance ended, he was in the passage leading from the boxes to the door, and he remarked that the young man, who, doubtless, observed the dress he wore, tried to conceal himself, as he passed him, by putting his handkerchief before his face. He followed him, at a distance, to the inn called the Vicomte de Turenne, which he saw him and the woman enter; and, being now certain of success, he ran to inform the Ambassador. The Marquis de St. Gilles immediately repaired to the inn, wrapped in a cloak, and followed by his page and two servants. He desired the landlord to show him to the room of a young man and woman, who had lodged for some time in his house. The landlord, for some time, refused to do so, unless the Marquis would give their name. The page told him to take notice that he was speaking to the Spanish Ambassador, who had strong reasons for wishing to see the persons in question. The innkeeper said they wished not to be known, and that they had absolutely forbidden him to admit anybody into their apartment who did not ask for them by name; but that, since the Ambassador desired it, he would show him their room. He then conducted them up to a dirty, miserable garret. He knocked at the door, and waited for some time; he then knocked again pretty, loudly, upon which the door was half-opened. At the sight of the Ambassador and his suite, the person who opened it immediately closed it again, exclaiming that they, had made a mistake. The Ambassador pushed hard against him, forced his way, in, made a sign to his people to wait outside, and remained in the room. He saw before him a very handsome young man, whose appearance perfectly, corresponded with the description, and a young woman, of great beauty, and remarkably fine person, whose countenance, form, colour of the hair, etc., were also precisely those described by the Count of Moncade. The young man spoke first. He complained of the violence used in breaking into the apartment of a stranger, living in a free country, and under the protection of its laws. The Ambassador stepped forward to embrace him, and said, 'It is useless to feign, my dear Count; I know you, and I do not come here — to give pain to you or to this lady, whose appearance interests me extremely.' The young man replied that he was totally mistaken; that he was not a Count, but the son of a merchant of Cadiz; that the lady was his wife; and, that they were travelling for pleasure. The Ambassador, casting his eyes round the miserably furnished room, which contained but one bed, and some packages of the shabbiest kind, lying in disorder about the room, 'Is this, my dear child (allow me to address you by a title which is warranted by my tender regard for your father), is this a fit residence for the son of the Count of Moncade?' The young man still protested against the use of any such language, as addressed to him. At length, overcome by the entreaties of the Ambassador, he confessed, weeping, that he was the son of the Count of Moncade, but declared that nothing should induce him to return to his father, if he must abandon a woman he adored. The young woman burst into tears, and threw herself at the feet of the Ambassador, telling him that she would not be the cause of the ruin of the young Count; and that generosity, or rather, love, would enable her to disregard her own happiness, and, for his sake, to separate herself from him. The Ambassador admired her noble disinterestedness. The young man, on the contrary, received her declaration with the most desperate grief. He reproached his mistress, and declared that he would never abandon so estimable a creature, nor suffer the sublime generosity of her heart to be turned against herself. The Ambassador told him that the Count of Moncade was far from wishing to render her miserable, and that he was commissioned to provide her with a sum sufficient to enable her to return into Spain, or to live where she liked. Her noble sentiments, and genuine tenderness, he said, inspired him with the greatest interest for her, and would induce him to go to the utmost limits of his powers, in the sum he was to give her; that he, therefore, promised her ten thousand florins, that is to say, about twelve hundred Louis, which would be given her the moment she surrendered the promise of marriage she had received, and the Count of Moncade took up his abode in the Ambassador's house, and promised to return to Spain. The young woman seemed perfectly indifferent to the sum proposed, and wholly absorbed in her lover, and in the grief of leaving him. She seemed insensible to everything but the cruel sacrifice which her reason, and her love itself, demanded. At length, drawing from a little portfolio the promise of marriage, signed by the Count, 'I know his heart too well,' said she, 'to need it.' Then she kissed it again and again, with a sort of transport, and delivered it to the Ambassador, who stood by, astonished at the grandeur of soul he witnessed. He promised her that he would never cease to take the liveliest interest in her fate, and assured the Count of his father's forgiveness. 'He will receive with open arms,' said he, 'the prodigal son, returning to the bosom of his distressed family; the heart of a father is an exhaustless mine of tenderness. How great will be the felicity of my friend on the receipt of these tidings, after his long anxiety and affliction; how happy do I esteem myself, at being the instrument of that felicity?' Such was, in part, the language of the Ambassador, which appeared to produce a strong impression on the young man. But, fearing lest, during the night, love should regain all his power, and should triumph over the generous resolution of the lady, the Marquis pressed the young Count to accompany him to his hotel. The tears, the cries of anguish, which marked this cruel separation, cannot be described; they deeply touched the heart of the Ambassador, who promised to watch over the young lady. The Count's little baggage was not difficult to remove, and, that very evening, he was installed in the finest apartment of the Ambassador's house. The Marquis was overjoyed at having restored to the illustrious house of Moncade the heir of its greatness, and of its magnificent domains. On the following morning, as soon as the young Count was up, he found tailors, dealers in cloth, lace, stuffs, etc., out of which he had only to choose. Two valets de chambre, and three laquais, chosen by the Ambassador for their intelligence and good conduct, were in waiting in his antechamber, and presented themselves, to receive his orders. The Ambassador shewed the young Count the letter he had just written to his father, in which he congratulated him on possessing a son whose noble sentiments and striking qualities were worthy of his illustrious blood, and announced his speedy return. The young lady was not forgotten; he confessed that to her generosity he was partly indebted for the submission of her lover, and expressed his conviction that the Count would not disapprove the gift he had made her, of ten thousand florins. That sum was remitted, on the same day, to this noble and interesting girl, who left the Hague without delay. The preparations for the Count's journey were made; a splendid wardrobe and an excellent carriage were embarked at Rotterdam, in a ship bound for France, on board which a passage was secured for the Count, who was to proceed from that country to Spain. A considerable sum of money, and letters of credit on Paris, were given him at his departure; and the parting between the Ambassador and the young Count was most touching. The Marquis de St. Gilles awaited with impatience the Count's answer, and enjoyed his friend's delight by anticipation. At the expiration of four months, he received this long-expected letter. It would be utterly impossible to describe his surprise on reading the following words, 'Heaven, my dear Marquis, never granted me the happiness of becoming a father, and, in the midst of abundant wealth and honours, the grief of having no heirs, and seeing an illustrious race end in my person, has shed the greatest bitterness over my whole existence. I see, with extreme regret, that you have been imposed upon by a young adventurer, who has taken advantage of the knowledge he had, by some means, obtained, of our old friendship. But your Excellency must not be the sufferer. The Count of Moncade is, most assuredly, the person whom you wished to serve; he is bound to repay what your generous friendship hastened to advance, in order to procure him a happiness which he would have felt most deeply. I hope, therefore, Marquis, that your Excellency will have no hesitation in accepting the remittance contained in this letter, of three thousand Louis of France, of the disbursal of which you sent me an account.'"

The manner in which the Comte de St. Germain spoke, in the characters of the young adventurer, his mistress, and the Ambassador, made his audience weep and laugh by turns. The story is true in every particular, and the adventurer surpasses Gusman d'Alfarache in address, according to the report of some persons present. Madame de Pompadour thought of having a play written, founded on this story; and the Count sent it to her in writing, from which I transcribed it.

M. Duclos came to the Doctor's, and harangued with his usual warmth. I heard him saying to two or three persons, "People are unjust to great men, Ministers and Princes; nothing, for instance, is more common than to undervalue their intellect. I astonished one of these little gentlemen of the corps of the infallibles, by telling him that I could prove that there had been more men of ability in the house of Bourbon, for the last hundred years, than in any other family."—"You prove that?" said somebody, sneeringly. "Yes," said Duclos; "and I will tell you how. The great Conde, you will allow, was no fool; and the Duchesse de Longueville is cited as one of the wittiest women that ever lived. The Regent was a man who had few equals, in every kind of talent and acquirement. The Prince de Conti, who was elected King of Poland, was celebrated for his intelligence, and, in poetry, was the successful rival of La Fare and St. Aulaire. The Duke of Burgundy was learned and enlightened. His Duchess, the daughter of Louis XIV., was remarkably clever, and wrote epigrams and couplets. The Duc du Maine is generally spoken of only for his weakness, but nobody had a more agreeable wit. His wife was mad, but she had an extensive acquaintance with letters, good taste in poetry, and a brilliant and inexhaustible imagination. Here are instances enough, I think," said he; "and, as I am no flatterer, and hate to appear one, I will not speak of the living." His hearers were astonished at this enumeration, and all of them agreed in the truth of what he had said. He added, "Don't we daily hear of silly D'Argenson,

[Rene LOUIS d'Argenson, who was Minister for Foreign Affairs. He was the author of 'Considerations sur le Gouvernement', and of several other works, from which succeeding political writers have drawn, and still draw ideas, which they give to the world as new. This man, remarkable not only for profound and original thinking, but for clear and forcible expression, was, nevertheless, D'Argenson la bete. It is said, however, that he affected the simplicity, and even silliness of manner, which procured him that appellation. If, as we hope, the unedited memoirs left by Rene d'Argenson will be given to the world, they will be found fully to justify the opinion of Duclos, with regard to this Minister, and the inappropriateness of his nickname.]

because he has a good-natured air, and a bourgeois tone? and yet, I believe, there have not been many Ministers comparable to him in knowledge and in enlightened views." I took a pen, which lay on the Doctor's table, and begged M. Duclos to repeat to me all the names he had mentioned, and the eulogium he had bestowed on each. "If," said he, "you show that to the Marquise, tell her how the conversation arose, and that I did not say it in order that it might come to her ears, and eventually, perhaps, to those of another person. I am an historiographer, and I will render justice, but I shall, also, often inflict it." — "I will answer for that," said the Doctor, "and our master will be represented as he really is. Louis XIV. liked verses, and patronised poets; that was very well, perhaps, in his time, because one must begin with something; but this age will be very superior to the last. It must be acknowledged that Louis XV., in sending astronomers to Mexico and Peru, to measure the earth, has a higher claim to our respect than if he directed an opera. He has thrown down the barriers which opposed the progress of philosophy, in spite of the clamour of the devotees: the Encyclopaedia will do honour to his reign." Duclos, during this speech, shook his head. I went away, and tried to write down all I had heard, while it was fresh. I had the part which related to the Princes of the Bourbon race copied by a valet, who wrote a beautiful hand, and I gave it to Madame de Pompadour. But she said to me, "What! is Duclos an acquaintance of yours? Do you want to play the 'bel esprit', my dear good woman? That will not sit well upon you." The truth is, that nothing can be further from my inclination. I told her that I met him accidentally at the Doctor's, where he generally spent an hour when he came to Versailles. "The King knows him to be a worthy man," said she.

Madame de Pompadour was ill, and the King came to see her several times a day. I generally left the room when he entered, but, having stayed a few minutes, on one occasion, to give her a glass of chicory water, I heard the King mention Madame d'Egmont. Madame raised her eyes to heaven, and said, "That name always recalls to me a most melancholy and barbarous affair; but it was not my fault." These words dwelt in my mind, and, particularly, the tone in which they were uttered. As I stayed with Madame till three o'clock in the morning, reading to her a part of the time, it was easy for me to try to satisfy my curiosity. I seized a moment, when the reading was interrupted, to say, "You looked dreadfully shocked, Madame, when the King pronounced the name of D'Egmont." At these words, she again raised her eyes, and said, "You would feel as I do, if you knew the affair."—"It must, then, be deeply affecting, for I do not think that it personally concerns you, Madame."—"No," said she, "it does not; as, however, I am not the only person acquainted with this history, and as I know you to be discreet, I will tell it you. The last Comte d'Egmont married a reputed daughter of the Duc de Villars; but the Duchess had never lived with her husband, and the Comtesse d'Egmont is, in fact, a daughter of the Chevalier d'Orleans.—[Legitimate son of the Regent, Grand Prior of France.]—At the death of her husband, young, beautiful, agreeable, and heiress to an immense fortune, she attracted the suit and homage of all the most distinguished men at Court. Her mother's director, one day, came into her room and requested a private interview; he then revealed to her that she was the offspring of an adulterous intercourse, for which her mother had been doing penance for five-and-twenty years. 'She could not,' said he, 'oppose your former marriage, although it caused her extreme distress. Heaven did not grant you children; but, if you marry again, you run the risk, Madame, of transmitting to another family the immense wealth, which does not, in fact, belong to you, and which is the price of crime.'

"The Comtesse d'Egmont heard this recital with horror. At the same instant, her mother entered, and, on her knees, besought her daughter to avert her eternal damnation. Madame d'Egmont tried to calm her own and her mother's mind. 'What can I do?' said she, to her. 'Consecrate yourself wholly to God,' replied the director, 'and thus expiate your mother's crime.' The Countess, in her terror, promised whatever they asked, and proposed to enter the Carmelites. I was informed of it, and spoke to the King about the barbarous tyranny the Duchesse de Villars and the director were about to exercise over this unhappy young woman; but we knew not how to prevent it. The King, with the utmost kindness, prevailed on the Queen to offer her the situation of Lady of the Palace, and desired the Duchess's friends to persuade her to endeavour to deter her daughter from becoming a Carmelite. It was all in vain; the wretched victim was sacrificed."

Madame took it into her head to consult a fortuneteller, called Madame Bontemps, who had told M. de Bernis's fortune, as I have already related, and had surprised him by her predictions. M. de Choiseul, to whom she mentioned the matter, said that the woman had also foretold fine things that were to happen to him. "I know it," said she, "and, in return, you promised her a carriage, but the poor woman goes on foot still." Madame told me this, and asked me how she could disguise herself, so as to see the woman without being known. I dared not propose any scheme then, for fear it should not succeed; but, two days after, I talked to her surgeon about the art, which some beggars practise, of counterfeiting sores, and altering their features. He said that was easy enough. I let the thing drop, and, after an interval of some minutes, I said, "If one could change one's features, one might have great diversion at the opera, or at balls. What alterations would it be necessary to make in me, now, to render it impossible to recognise me?"—"In the first place," said he, "you must alter the colour of your hair, then you must have a false nose, and put a spot on some part of your face, or a wart, or a few hairs." I laughed, and said, "Help me to contrive this for the next ball; I have not been to one for twenty years; but I am dying to puzzle somebody, and to tell him things which no one but I can tell him. I shall come home, and go to bed, in a quarter of an hour."—"I must take the measure of your nose," said he; "or do you take it with wax, and I will have a nose made: you can get a flaxen or brown wig." I repeated to Madame what the surgeon had told me: she was delighted at it. I took the measure of her nose, and of my own, and carried them to the surgeon, who, in two days, gave me the two noses, and a wart, which Madame stuck under her left eye, and some paint for the eyebrows. The noses were most delicately made, of a bladder, I think, and these, with the ether disguises, rendered it impossible to recognize the face, and yet did not produce any shocking appearance. All this being accomplished, nothing remained but to give notice to the fortuneteller; we waited for a little excursion to Paris, which Madame was to take, to look at her house. I then got a person, with whom I had no connection, to speak to a waiting-woman of the Duchesse de Ruffec, to obtain an interview with the woman. She made some difficulty, on account of the Police; but we promised secrecy, and appointed the place of meeting. Nothing could be more contrary to Madame de Pompadour's character, which was one of extreme timidity, than to engage in such an adventure. But her curiosity was raised to the highest pitch, and, moreover, everything was so well arranged that there was not the slightest risk. Madame had let M. de Gontaut, and her valet de chambre, into the secret. The latter had hired two rooms for his niece, who was then ill, at Versailles, near Madame's hotel. We went out in the evening, followed by the valet de chambre, who was a safe man, and by the Duke, all on foot. We had not, at farthest, above two hundred steps to go. We were shown into two small rooms, in which were fires. The two men remained in one, and we in the other. Madame had thrown herself on a sofa. She had on a night-cap, which concealed half her face, in an unstudied manner. I was near the fire, leaning on a table, on which were two candles. There were lying on the chairs, near us, some clothes, of small value. The fortune-teller rang—a little servant-girl let her in, and then went to wait in the room where the gentlemen were. Coffee-cups, and a coffee-pot, were set; and I had taken care to place, upon a little buffet, some cakes, and a bottle of Malaga wine, having heard that Madame Bontemps assisted her inspiration with that liquor. Her face, indeed, sufficiently proclaimed it. "Is that lady ill?" said she, seeing Madame de Pompadour stretched languidly on the sofa. I told her that she would soon be better, but that she had kept her room for a week. She heated the coffee, and prepared the two cups, which she carefully wiped, observing that nothing impure must enter into this operation. I affected to be very anxious for a glass of wine, in order to give our oracle a pretext for assuaging her thirst, which she did, without much entreaty. When she had drunk two or three small glasses (for I had taken care not to have large ones), she poured the coffee into one of the two large cups. "This is yours," said she; "and this is your friends's; let them stand a little." She then observed our hands and our faces; after which she drew a looking-glass from her pocket, into which she told us to look, while she looked at the reflections of our faces. She next took a glass of wine, and immediately threw herself into a fit of enthusiasm, while she inspected my cup, and considered all the lines formed by the dregs of the coffee she had poured out. She began by saying, "That is well—prosperity—but there is a black mark—distresses. A man becomes a comforter. Here, in this corner, are friends, who support you. Ah! who is he that persecutes them? But justice triumphs— after rain, sunshine—a long journey successful. There, do you see these little bags? That is money which has been paid—to you, of course, I mean. That is well. Do you see that arm?"—"Yes."—"That is an arm supporting something: a woman veiled; I see her; it is you.

All this is clear to me. I hear, as it were, a voice speaking to me. You are no longer attacked. I see it, because the clouds in that direction are passed off (pointing to a clearer spot). But, stay—I see small lines which branch out from the main spot. These are sons, daughters, nephews—that is pretty well." She appeared overpowered with the effort she was making. At length, she added, "That is all. You have had good luck first—misfortune afterward. You have had a friend, who has exerted himself with success to extricate you from it. You have had lawsuits—at length fortune has been reconciled to you, and will change no more." She drank another glass of wine. "Your health, Madame," said she to the Marquise, and went through the same ceremonies with the cup. At length, she broke out, "Neither fair nor foul. I see there, in the distance, a serene sky; and then all these things that appear to ascend all these things are applauses. Here is a grave man, who stretches out his arms. Do you see?—look attentively."—"That is true," said Madame de Pompadour, with surprise (there was, indeed, some appearance of the kind). "He points to something square that is an open coffer. Fine weather. But, look! there are clouds of azure and gold, which surround you. Do you see that ship on the high sea? How favourable the wind is! You are on board; you land in a beautiful country, of which you become the Queen. Ah! what do I see? Look there—look at that hideous, crooked, lame man, who is pursuing you—but he is going on a fool's errand. I see a very great man, who supports you in his arms. Here, look! he is a kind of giant. There is a great deal of gold and silver—a few clouds here and there. But you have nothing to fear. The vessel will be sometimes tossed about, but it will not be lost. Dixi." Madame said, "When shall I die, and of what disease?"—"I never speak of that," said she; "see here, rather but fate will not permit it. I will shew you how fate confounds everything"—shewing her several confused lumps of the coffee-dregs. "Well, never mind as to the time, then, only tell me the kind of death." The fortune-teller looked in the cup, and said, "You will have time to prepare yourself." I gave her only two Louis, to avoid doing anything remarkable. She left us, after begging us to keep her secret, and we rejoined the Duc de Gontaut, to whom we related everything that had passed. He laughed heartily, and said, "Her coffee-dregs are like the clouds—you may see what you please in them."

There was one thing in my horoscope which struck me, that was the comforter; because one of my uncles had taken great care of me, and had rendered me the most essential services. It is also true that I afterwards had an important lawsuit; and, lastly, there was the money which had come into my hands through Madame de Pompadour's patronage and bounty. As for Madame, her husband was represented accurately enough by the man with the coffer; then the country of which she became Queen seemed to relate to her present situation at Court; but the most remarkable thing was the crooked and lame man, in whom Madame thought she recognized the Duc de V— —-, who was very much deformed. Madame was delighted with her adventure and her horoscope, which she thought corresponded very remarkably with the truth. Two days after, she sent for M. de St. Florentin, and begged him not to molest the fortuneteller. He laughed, and replied that he knew why she interceded for this woman. Madame asked him why he laughed. He related every circumstance of her expedition with astonishing exactness;— [M. de St. Florentin was Minister for Paris, to whom the Lieutenant of Police was accountable.]—but he knew nothing of what had been said, or, at least, so he pretended. He promised Madame that, provided Bontemps did nothing which called for notice, she should not be obstructed in the exercise of her profession, especially if she followed it in secret. "I know her," added he, "and I, like other people, have had the curiosity to consult her. She is the wife of a soldier in the guards. She is a clever woman in her way, but she drinks. Four or five years ago, she got such hold on the mind of Madame de Ruffec, that she made her believe she could procure her an elixir of beauty, which would restore her to what she was at twenty-five. The Duchess pays high for the drugs of which this elixir is compounded; and sometimes they are bad: sometimes, the sun, to which they were exposed, was not powerful enough; sometimes, the influence of a certain constellation was wanting. Sometimes, she has the courage to assure the Duchess that she really is grown handsomer, and actually succeeds in making her believe it." But the history of this woman's daughter is still more curious. She was exquisitely beautiful, and the Duchess brought her up in her own house. Bontemps predicted to the girl, in the Duchess's presence, that she would marry a man of two thousand Louis a year. This was not very likely to happen to the daughter of a soldier in the guards.

It did happen, nevertheless. The little Bontemps married the President Beaudouin, who was mad. But, the tragical part of the story is, that her mother had also foretold that she would die in childbirth of her first child, and that she did actually die in child-birth, at the age of eighteen, doubtless under a strong impression of her mother's prophecy, to which the improbable event of her marriage had given such extraordinary weight. Madame told the King of the adventure her curiosity had led her into, at which he laughed, and said he wished the Police had arrested her. He added a very sensible remark. "In order to judge," said he, "of the truth or falsehood of such predictions, one ought to collect fifty of them. It would be found that they are almost always made up of the same phrases, which are sometimes inapplicable, and some times hit the mark. But the first are rarely-mentioned, while the others are always insisted on."

I have heard, and, indeed, it is certainly true, that M. de Bridge lived on terms of intimacy with Madame, when she was Madame d'Aioles. He used to ride on horseback with her, and, as he is so handsome a man, that he has retained the name of the handsome man, it was natural enough that he should be thought the lover of a very handsome woman. I have heard something more than this. I was told that the King said to M. de Bridge, "Confess, now, that you were her lover. She has acknowledged it to me, and I exact from you this proof of sincerity." M. de. Bridge replied, that Madame de Pompadour was at liberty to say what she pleased for her own amusement, or for any other reason; but that he, for his part, could not assert a falsehood; that he had been, her friend; that she was a charming companion, and had great talents; that he delighted in her society; but that his intercourse with her had never gone beyond the bounds of friendship. He added, that her husband was present in all their parties, that he watched her with a jealous eye, and that he would not have suffered him to be so much with her if he had conceived the least suspicion of the kind. The King persisted, and told him he was wrong to endeavour to conceal a fact which was unquestionable. It was rumoured, also, that the Abbe de Bernis had been a favoured lover of hers. The said Abbe was rather a coxcomb; he had a handsome face, and wrote poetry. Madame de Pompadour was the theme of his gallant verses. He sometimes received the compliments of his friends upon his success with a smile which left some room for conjecture, although he denied the thing in words. It was, for some time, reported at Court that she was in love with the Prince de Beauvau: he is a man distinguished for his gallantries, his air of rank and fashion, and his high play; he is brother to the little Marechale: for all these reasons, Madame is very civil to him, but there is nothing marked in her behaviour. She knows, besides, that he is in love with a very agreeable woman.

Now that I am on the subject of lovers, I cannot avoid speaking of M. de Choiseul. Madame likes him better than any of those I have just mentioned, but he is not her lover. A lady, whom I know perfectly well, but whom I do not chose to denounce to Madame, invented a story about them, which was utterly false. She said, as I have good reason to believe, that one day, hearing the King coming, I ran to Madame's closet door; that I coughed in a particular manner; and that the King having, happily, stopped a moment to talk to some ladies, there was time to adjust matters, so that Madame came out of the closet with me and M. de Choiseul, as if we had been all three sitting together. It is very true that I went in to carry something to Madame, without knowing that the King was come, and that she came out of the closet with M. de Choiseul, who had a paper in his hand, and that I followed her a few minutes after. The King asked M. de Choiseul what that paper was which he had in his hand. He replied that it contained the remonstrance from the Parliament.

Three or four ladies witnessed what I now relate, and as, with the exception of one, they were all excellent women, and greatly attached to Madame, my suspicions could fall on none but the one in question, whom I will not name, because her brother has always treated me with great kindness. Madame de Pompadour had a lively imagination and great sensibility, but nothing could exceed the coldness of her temperament. It would, besides, have been extremely difficult for her, surrounded as she was, to keep up an intercourse of that kind with any man. It is true that this difficulty would have been diminished in the case of an all-powerful Minister, who had constant pretexts for seeing her in private. But there was a much more decisive fact—M. de Choiseul had a charming mistress—the Princess de R———, and Madame knew it, and often spoke of her. He had, besides, some remains of liking for the Princess de Kinski, who followed him from Vienna. It is true that he soon after discovered how ridiculous she was. All these circumstances combined were, surely, sufficient to deter Madame from engaging in a love affair with the Duke; but his talents and agreeable qualities captivated her. He was not handsome, but he had manners peculiar to himself, an agreeable vivacity, a delightful gaiety; this was the general opinion of his character. He was much attached to Madame, and though this might, at first, be inspired by a consciousness of the importance of her friendship to his interest, yet, after he had acquired sufficient political strength to stand alone, he was not the less devoted to her, nor less assiduous in his attentions. He knew her friendship for me, and he one day said to me, with great feeling, "I am afraid, my dear Madame du Hausset, that she will sink into a state of complete dejection, and die of melancholy. Try to divert her." What a fate for the favourite of the greatest monarch in existence! thought I.

One day, Madame de Pompadour had retired to her closet with M. Berryer. Madame d'Amblimont stayed with Madame de Gontaut, who called me to talk about my son. A moment after, M. de Gontaut came in and said, "D'Amblimont, who shall have the Swiss guards?" — "Stop a moment," said she; "let me call my council — —, M. de Choiseul." — "That is not so very bad a thought," said M. de Gontaut, "but I assure you, you are the first person who has suggested it." He immediately left us, and Madame d'Amblimont said, "I'll lay a wager he is going to communicate my idea to M. de Choiseul." He returned very shortly, and, M. Berrier having left the room, he said to Madame de Pompadour, "A singular thought has entered d'Amblimont's head." — "What absurdity now?" said Madame. "Not so great an absurdity neither," said he. "She says the Swiss guards ought to be given to M. de Choiseul, and, really, if the King has not positively promised M. de Soubise, I don't see what he can do better." — "The King has promised nothing," said Madame, "and the hopes I gave him were of the vaguest kind. I only told him it was possible. But though I have a great regard for M. de Soubise, I do not think his merits comparable to those of M. de Choiseul." When the King came in, Madame, doubtless, told him of this suggestion. A quarter of an hour afterwards, I went into the room to speak to her, and I heard the King say, "You will see that, because

the Duc du Maine, and his children, had that place, he will think he
ought to have it, on account of his rank as Prince (Soubise); but the
Marechal de Bassompierre was not a Prince; and, by the bye, the
Duc de Choiseul is his grandnephew; do you know that?"—"Your
Majesty is better acquainted with the history of France than anybody," replied Madame. Two days after this, Madame de said to
me, "I have two great delights; M. de Soubise will not have the
Swiss guards, and Madame de Marsan will be ready to burst with
rage at it; this is the first: and M. de Choiseul will have them; this is
the greatest."

....

[The whole of this passage is in a different handwriting.]

There was a universal talk of a young lady with whom the King
was as much in love as it was possible for him to be. Her name was
Romans. She was said to be a charming girl. Madame de Pompadour knew of the King's visits, and her confidantes brought her
most alarming reports of the affair. The Marechale de Mirepoix,
who had the best head in Madame's council, was the only one who
encouraged her. "I do not tell you," said she, "that he loves you better than her; and if she could be transported hither by the stroke of a
fairy's wand; if she could entertain him this evening at supper; if
she were familiar with all his tastes, there would, perhaps, be sufficient reason for you to tremble for your power. But Princes are,
above all, pre-eminently the slaves of habit. The King's attachment
to you is like that he bears to your apartment, your furniture. You
have formed yourself to his manners and habits; you know how to
listen and reply to his stories; he is under no constraint with you; he
has no fear of boring you. How do you think he could have resolution to uproot all this in a day, to form a new establishment, and to
make a public exhibition of himself by so striking a change in his
arrangements?" The young lady became pregnant; the reports cur-
rent among the people, and even those at Court, alarmed Madame
dreadfully. It was said that the King meant to legitimate the child,
and to give the mother a title. "All that," said Madame de Mirepoix,
"is in the style of Louis XIV.—such dignified proceedings are very
unlike those of our master." Mademoiselle Romans lost all her influence over the King by her indiscreet boasting. She was even treated

with harshness and violence, which were in no degree instigated by Madame. Her house was searched, and her papers seized; but the most important, those which substantiated the fact of the King's paternity, had been withdrawn. At length she gave birth to a son, who was christened under the name of Bourbon, son of Charles de Bourbon, Captain of Horse. The mother thought the eyes of all France were fixed upon her, and beheld in her son a future Duc du Maine. She suckled him herself, and she used to carry him in a sort of basket to the Bois de Boulogne. Both mother and child were covered with the finest laces. She sat down upon the grass in a solitary spot, which, however, was soon well known, and there gave suck to her royal babe. Madame had great curiosity to see her, and took me, one day, to the manufactory at Sevres, without telling me what she projected. After she had bought some cups, she said, "I want to go and walk in the Bois de Boulogne," and gave orders to the coachman to stop at a certain spot where she wished to alight. She had got the most accurate directions, and when she drew near the young lady's haunt she gave me her arm, drew her bonnet over her eyes, and held her pocket-handkerchief before the lower part of her face. We walked, for some minutes, in a path, from whence we could see the lady suckling her child. Her jet black hair was turned up, and confined by a diamond comb. She looked earnestly at us. Madame bowed to her, and whispered to me, pushing me by the elbow, "Speak to her." I stepped forward, and exclaimed, "What a lovely child!"—"Yes, Madame," replied she, "I must confess that he is, though I am his mother." Madame, who had hold of my arm, trembled, and I was not very firm. Mademoiselle Romans said to me, "Do you live in this neighbourhood?"—"Yes, Madame," replied I, "I live at Auteuil with this lady, who is just now suffering from a most dreadful toothache."—"I pity her sincerely, for I know that tormenting pain well." I looked all around, for fear any one should come up who might recognise us. I took courage to ask her whether the child's father was a handsome man. "Very handsome, and, if I told you his name, you would agree with me."—"I have the honour of knowing him, then, Madame?"—"Most probably you do." Madame, fearing, as I did, some rencontre, said a few words in a low tone, apologizing for having intruded upon her, and we took our leave. We looked behind us, repeatedly, to see if we were followed, and got into the carriage without being perceived. "It must be confessed that both mother and child are beautiful creatures," said Madame — "not to mention the father; the infant has his eyes. If the King had come up while we were there, do you think he would have recognised us?" — "I don't doubt that he would, Madame, and then what an agitation I should have been in, and what a scene it would have been for the bystanders! and, above all, what a surprise to her!" In the evening, Madame made the King a present of the cups she had bought, but she did not mention her walk, for fear Mademoiselle Romans should tell him that two ladies, who knew him, had met her there such a day. Madame de Mirepoix said to Madame, "Be assured, the King cares very little about children; he has enough of them, and he will not be troubled with the mother or the son. See what sort of notice he takes of the Comte de I — — -, who is strikingly like him. He never speaks of him, and I am convinced that he will never do anything for him. Again and again I tell you, we do not live under Louis XIV." Madame de Mirepoix had been Ambassadress to London, and had often heard the English make this remark.

Some alterations had been made in Madame de Pompadour's rooms, and I had no longer, as heretofore, the niche in which I had been permitted to sit, to hear Caffarelli, and, in later times, Mademoiselle Fel and Jeliotte. I, therefore, went more frequently to my lodgings in town, where I usually received my friends: more particularly when Madame visited her little hermitage, whither M. de Gontaut commonly accompanied her. Madame du Chiron, the wife of the Head Clerk in the War-Office, came to see me. "I feel," said she, "greatly embarrassed, in speaking to you about an affair, which will, perhaps, embarrass you also. This is the state of the case. A very poor woman, to whom I have sometimes given a little assistance, pretends to be a relation of the Marquise de Pompadour. Here is her petition." I read it, and said that the woman had better write directly to Madame, and that I was sure, if what she asserted was true, her application would be successful. Madame du Chiron followed my advice. The woman wrote she was in the lowest depth of poverty, and I learnt that Madame sent her six Louis until she could gain more accurate information as to the truth of her story. Colin, who was commissioned to take the money, made inquiries of M. de Malvoiain, a relation of Madame, and a very respectable officer. The fact was found to be as she had stated it. Madame then sent her a hundred louis, and promised her a pension of sixty louis a year. All this was done with great expedition, and Madame had a visit of thanks from her poor relation, as soon as she had procured decent clothes to come in. That day the King happened to come in at an unusual hour, and saw this person going out. He asked who it was. "It is a very poor relation of mine," replied Madame. "She came, then, to beg for some assistance?"—"No," said she. "What did she come for, then?"—"To thank me for a little service I have rendered her," said she, blushing from the fear of seeming to boast of her liberality. "Well," said the King; "since she is your relation, allow me to have the pleasure of serving her too. I will give her fifty louis a year out of my private purse, and, you know, she may send for the first year's allowance to-morrow." Madame burst into tears, and kissed the King's hand several times. She told me this three days afterwards, when I was nursing her in a slight attack of fever. I could not refrain from weeping myself at this instance of the King's kindness. The next day, I called on Madame du Chiron to tell her of the good fortune of her protege; I forgot to say that, after Madame had related the affair to me, I told her what part I had taken in it. She approved my conduct, and allowed me to inform my friend of the King's goodness. This action, which showed no less delicate politeness towards her than sensibility to the sufferings of the poor woman, made a deeper impression on Madame's heart than a pension of two thousand a year given to herself.

Madame had terrible palpitations of the heart. Her heart actually seemed to leap. She consulted several physicians. I recollect that one of them made her walk up and down the room, lift a weight, and move quickly. On her expressing some surprise, he said, "I do this to ascertain whether the organ is diseased; in that case motion quickens the pulsation; if that effect is not produced, the complaint proceeds from the nerves." I repeated this to my oracle, Quesnay. He knew very little of this physician, but he said his treatment was that of a clever man. His name was Renard; he was scarcely known beyond the Marais. Madame often appeared suffocated, and sighed continually. One day, under pretence of presenting a petition to M. de Choiseul, as he was going out, I said, in a low voice, that I wished to see him a few minutes on an affair of importance to my mistress. He told me to come as soon as I pleased, and that I should be admitted. I told him that Madame was extremely depressed; that she gave way to distressing thoughts, which she would not communicate; that she, one day, said to me, "The fortune-teller told me I should have time to prepare myself; I believe it, for I shall be worn to death by melancholy." M. de Choiseul appeared much affected; he praised my zeal, and said that he had already perceived some indications of what I told him; that he would not mention my name, but would try to draw from her an explanation. I don't know what he said to her; but, from that time, she was much more calm. One day, but long afterwards, Madame said to M. de Gontaut, "I am generally thought to have great influence, but if it were not for M. de Choiseul, I should not be able to obtain a Cross of St. Louis."

The King and Madame de Pompadour had a very high opinion of Madame de Choiseul. Madame said, "She always says the right thing in the right place." Madame de Grammont was not so agreeable to them; and I think that this was to be attributed, in part, to the sound of her voice, and to her blunt manner of speaking; for she was said to be a woman of great sense, and devotedly attached to the King and Madame de Pompadour. Some people pretended that she tried to captivate the King, and to supplant Madame: nothing could be more false, or more ridiculously improbable. Madame saw a great deal of these two ladies, who were extremely attentive to her. She one day remarked to the Duc d'Ayen,—[Afterwards Marechal de Noaines.] that M. de Choiseul was very fond of his sisters. "I know it, Madame," said he, "and many sisters are the better for that."—"What do you mean?" said she. "Why," said he, "as the Duc de Choiseul loves his sister, it is thought fashionable to do the same; and I know silly girls, whose brothers formerly cared nothing about them, who are now most tenderly beloved. No sooner does their little finger ache, than their brothers are running about to fetch physicians from all corners of Paris. They flatter themselves that somebody will say, in M. de Choiseul's drawing-room, 'How passionately M. de — — — loves his sister; he would certainly die if he had the misfortune to lose her.'" Madame related this to her brother, in my presence, adding, that she could not give it in the Duke's comic manner. M. de Marigny said, "I have had the start of them all, without making so much noise; and my dear little sister knows that I loved her tenderly before Madame de Grammont left her convent.

The Duc d'Ayen, however, is not very wrong; he has made the most of it in his lively manner, but it is partly true."—"I forgot," replied Madame, "that the Duke said, 'I want extremely to be in the fashion, but which sister shall I take up? Madame de Caumont is a devil incarnate, Madame de Villars drinks, Madame d'Armagnac is a bore, Madame de la Marck is half mad.'"—"These are fine family portraits, Duke," said Madame. The Duc de Gontaut laughed, during the whole of this conversation, immoderately. Madame repeated it, one day, when she kept her bed. M. de G——- also began to talk of his sister, Madame du Roure. I think, at least, that is the name he mentioned. He was very gay, and had the art of creating gaiety. Somebody said, he is an excellent piece of furniture for a favourite. He makes her laugh, and asks for nothing either for himself or for others; he cannot excite jealousy, and he meddles in nothing. He was called the White Eunuch. Madame's illness increased so rapidly that we were alarmed about her; but bleeding in the foot cured her as if by a miracle. The King watched her with the greatest solicitude; and I don't know whether his attentions did not contribute as much to the cure as the bleeding. M. de Choiseul remarked, some days after, that she appeared in better spirits. I told him that I thought this improvement might be attributed to the same cause.